D1739267

BELONGS TO:

....

....

PARK VISIT # ☐ DATE: ....

NATIONAL PARK: ....

CITY: .... **STATE:** ....

WENT WITH:

....

WEATHER:

....

INITIAL IMPRESSION:

....

LENGTH OF STAY:

....

EXPERIENCES/ OBSERVATIONS

FAVORITE MOMENT: ....

....

WILDLIFE SCENERY OBSERVED

....

....

....

PARK RATING 0/10

(1) (2) (3) (4) (5) (6) (7) (8) (9) (10)

WILL I VISIT AGAIN?   ◯ YES   ◯ NO

HIKING TRAIL: ....

LOCATION: ....

DATE: .... **DISTANCE:** ....

COMPANIONS: ....

WEATHER:

TRAIL DIFFICULTY:

○☀ ○☁ ○🌧

TEMPERATURE: ....

① ② ③ ④ ⑤

THOUGHTS ABOUT THIS HIKE

....

....

....

....

....

....

....

OVERALL RATING

☆ ☆ ☆ ☆ ☆

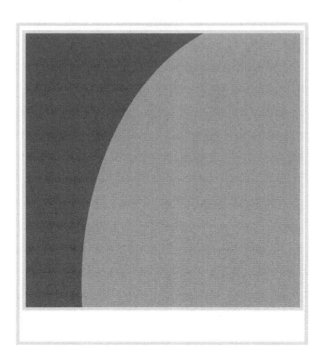

NOTES-MEMORIES-PHOTOS

....

....

....

....

....

....

....

....

....

....

SOUVENIRS TICKET STUBS MAPS MORE PICS

PARK VISIT # ☐ DATE: ....

NATIONAL PARK: ....

CITY: .... **STATE:** ....

WENT WITH: **INITIAL IMPRESSION:**

....

WEATHER: **LENGTH OF STAY:**

....

EXPERIENCES/ OBSERVATIONS

FAVORITE MOMENT: ....

....

WILDLIFE SCENERY OBSERVED

....

....

....

PARK RATING 0/10

(1) (2) (3) (4) (5) (6) (7) (8) (9) (10)

WILL I VISIT AGAIN? ◯ YES ◯ NO

HIKING TRAIL: ....

LOCATION: ....

DATE: ....   **DISTANCE:** ....

COMPANIONS: ....

WEATHER: TRAIL DIFFICULTY:

TEMPERATURE: ....   ① ② ③ ④ ⑤

THOUGHTS ABOUT THIS HIKE

....

....

....

....

....

....

....

OVERALL RATING

☆ ☆ ☆ ☆ ☆

NOTES-MEMORIES-PHOTOS

....

....

....

....

....

....

....

....

....

....

SOUVENIRS TICKET STUBS MAPS MORE PICS

PARK VISIT # ☐   **DATE:** ....

NATIONAL PARK: ....

CITY: ....   **STATE:** ....

WENT WITH: **INITIAL IMPRESSION:**

....

WEATHER: **LENGTH OF STAY:**

....

EXPERIENCES/ OBSERVATIONS

FAVORITE MOMENT: ....

....

WILDLIFE SCENERY OBSERVED

....

....

....

PARK RATING 0/10

(1) (2) (3) (4) (5) (6) (7) (8) (9) (10)

WILL I VISIT AGAIN?   ◯ **YES**   ◯ **NO**

HIKING TRAIL: ....

LOCATION: ....

DATE: .... **DISTANCE:** ....

COMPANIONS: ....

WEATHER:

TRAIL DIFFICULTY:

☀ ○ ☁ ○ 🌧

TEMPERATURE: ....

① ② ③ ④ ⑤

THOUGHTS ABOUT THIS HIKE

....

....

....

....

....

....

....

OVERALL RATING

☆ ☆ ☆ ☆ ☆

NOTES-MEMORIES-PHOTOS

....

....

....

....

....

....

....

....

....

....

SOUVENIRS TICKET STUBS MAPS MORE PICS

PARK VISIT # ☐ DATE: ....

NATIONAL PARK: ....

CITY: .... **STATE:** ....

WENT WITH: **INITIAL IMPRESSION:**

....

WEATHER: **LENGTH OF STAY:**

....

EXPERIENCES/ OBSERVATIONS

FAVORITE MOMENT: ....

....

WILDLIFE SCENERY OBSERVED

....

....

....

PARK RATING 0/10

① ② ③ ④ ⑤ ⑥ ⑦ ⑧ ⑨ ⑩

WILL I VISIT AGAIN? ◯ YES ◯ NO

HIKING TRAIL: ....

LOCATION: ....

DATE: ....   **DISTANCE:** ....

COMPANIONS: ....

WEATHER: ## TRAIL DIFFICULTY:

TEMPERATURE: ....   ① ② ③ ④ ⑤

THOUGHTS ABOUT THIS HIKE

....

....

....

....

....

....

....

OVERALL RATING

☆ ☆ ☆ ☆ ☆

NOTES-MEMORIES-PHOTOS

....

....

....

....

....

....

....

....

....

....

SOUVENIRS TICKET STUBS MAPS MORE PICS

PARK VISIT # ☐   DATE: ....

NATIONAL PARK: ....

CITY: ....   **STATE:** ....

WENT WITH: **INITIAL IMPRESSION:**

....

WEATHER: **LENGTH OF STAY:**

....

EXPERIENCES/ OBSERVATIONS

FAVORITE MOMENT: ....

....

WILDLIFE SCENERY OBSERVED

....

....

....

PARK RATING 0/10

(1) (2) (3) (4) (5) (6) (7) (8) (9) (10)

WILL I VISIT AGAIN?   ◯ YES   ◯ NO

HIKING TRAIL: ....

LOCATION: ....

DATE: .... **DISTANCE:** ....

COMPANIONS: ....

WEATHER:

TRAIL DIFFICULTY:

○ ☀ ○ ☁ ○ 🌧

1 2 3 4 5

TEMPERATURE: ....

THOUGHTS ABOUT THIS HIKE

....

....

....

....

....

....

....

OVERALL RATING

☆ ☆ ☆ ☆ ☆

NOTES-MEMORIES-PHOTOS

....

....

....

....

....

....

....

....

....

....

SOUVENIRS TICKET STUBS MAPS MORE PICS

PARK VISIT # ☐   DATE: ....

NATIONAL PARK: ....

CITY: ....   **STATE:** ....

WENT WITH: **INITIAL IMPRESSION:**

....

WEATHER: **LENGTH OF STAY:**

....

EXPERIENCES/ OBSERVATIONS

FAVORITE MOMENT: ....

....

WILDLIFE SCENERY OBSERVED

....

....

....

PARK RATING 0/10

(1) (2) (3) (4) (5) (6) (7) (8) (9) (10)

WILL I VISIT AGAIN?   ◯ YES   ◯ NO

HIKING TRAIL: ....

LOCATION: ....

DATE: .... **DISTANCE:** ....

COMPANIONS: ....

WEATHER:

TRAIL DIFFICULTY:

○ ☀ ○ ☁ ○ 🌧

TEMPERATURE: ....

(1) (2) (3) (4) (5)

THOUGHTS ABOUT THIS HIKE

....

....

....

....

....

....

....

OVERALL RATING

☆ ☆ ☆ ☆ ☆

NOTES-MEMORIES-PHOTOS

....

....

....

....

....

....

....

....

....

....

SOUVENIRS TICKET STUBS MAPS MORE PICS

PARK VISIT # ☐   DATE: ....

NATIONAL PARK: ....

CITY: ....   **STATE:** ....

WENT WITH: **INITIAL IMPRESSION:**

....

WEATHER: **LENGTH OF STAY:**

....

EXPERIENCES/ OBSERVATIONS

FAVORITE MOMENT: ....

....

WILDLIFE SCENERY OBSERVED

....

....

....

PARK RATING 0/10

(1) (2) (3) (4) (5) (6) (7) (8) (9) (10)

WILL I VISIT AGAIN?   ◯ YES   ◯ NO

HIKING TRAIL: ....

LOCATION: ....

DATE: .... **DISTANCE:** ....

COMPANIONS: ....

WEATHER:

☁☀ ☁☁ ☁🌧

TEMPERATURE: ....

TRAIL DIFFICULTY:

① ② ③ ④ ⑤

THOUGHTS ABOUT THIS HIKE

....

....

....

....

....

....

....

OVERALL RATING

☆ ☆ ☆ ☆ ☆

NOTES-MEMORIES-PHOTOS

....

....

....

....

....

....

....

....

....

....

SOUVENIRS TICKET STUBS MAPS MORE PICS

PARK VISIT # ☐   DATE: ....

NATIONAL PARK: ....

CITY: ....   **STATE:** ....

WENT WITH: **INITIAL IMPRESSION:**

....

WEATHER: **LENGTH OF STAY:**

....

EXPERIENCES/ OBSERVATIONS

FAVORITE MOMENT: ....

....

WILDLIFE SCENERY OBSERVED

....

....

....

PARK RATING 0/10

(1) (2) (3) (4) (5) (6) (7) (8) (9) (10)

WILL I VISIT AGAIN?   ◯ YES   ◯ NO

HIKING TRAIL: ....

LOCATION: ....

DATE: .... **DISTANCE:** ....

COMPANIONS: ....

WEATHER:

TRAIL DIFFICULTY:

⚬☀ ⚬☁ ⚬🌧

TEMPERATURE: ....

① ② ③ ④ ⑤

THOUGHTS ABOUT THIS HIKE

....

....

....

....

....

....

....

OVERALL RATING

☆ ☆ ☆ ☆ ☆

NOTES-MEMORIES-PHOTOS

....

....

....

....

....

....

....

....

....

....

SOUVENIRS TICKET STUBS MAPS MORE PICS

PARK VISIT # ☐   DATE: ....

NATIONAL PARK: ....

CITY: ....   **STATE:** ....

WENT WITH: **INITIAL IMPRESSION:**

....

WEATHER: **LENGTH OF STAY:**

....

EXPERIENCES/ OBSERVATIONS

FAVORITE MOMENT: ....

....

WILDLIFE SCENERY OBSERVED

....

....

....

PARK RATING 0/10

(1) (2) (3) (4) (5) (6) (7) (8) (9) (10)

WILL I VISIT AGAIN?   ◯ YES   ◯ NO

HIKING TRAIL: ....

LOCATION: ....

DATE: .... **DISTANCE:** ....

COMPANIONS: ....

WEATHER:

○ ☀ ○ ☁ ○ 🌧

TEMPERATURE: ....

TRAIL DIFFICULTY:

(1) (2) (3) (4) (5)

THOUGHTS ABOUT THIS HIKE

....

....

....

....

....

....

....

OVERALL RATING

☆ ☆ ☆ ☆ ☆

NOTES-MEMORIES-PHOTOS

....

....

....

....

....

....

....

....

....

....

SOUVENIRS TICKET STUBS MAPS MORE PICS

PARK VISIT # ⬭   DATE: ....

NATIONAL PARK: ....

CITY: ....   **STATE:** ....

WENT WITH: **INITIAL IMPRESSION:**

....

WEATHER: **LENGTH OF STAY:**

....

EXPERIENCES/ OBSERVATIONS

FAVORITE MOMENT: ....

....

WILDLIFE SCENERY OBSERVED

....

....

....

PARK RATING 0/10

(1) (2) (3) (4) (5) (6) (7) (8) (9) (10)

WILL I VISIT AGAIN?   ◯ YES   ◯ NO

HIKING TRAIL: ....

LOCATION: ....

DATE: ....   **DISTANCE:** ....

COMPANIONS: ....

WEATHER: TRAIL DIFFICULTY:

TEMPERATURE: ....

① ② ③ ④ ⑤

THOUGHTS ABOUT THIS HIKE

....
....
....
....
....
....
....

OVERALL RATING

☆☆☆☆☆

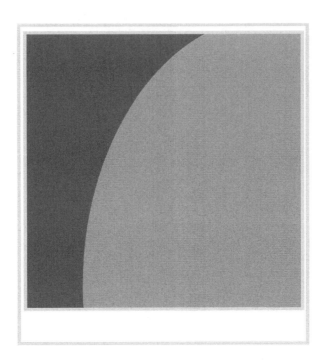

NOTES-MEMORIES-PHOTOS

....

....

....

....

....

....

....

....

....

....

SOUVENIRS TICKET STUBS MAPS MORE PICS

PARK VISIT # ☐   DATE: ....

NATIONAL PARK: ....

CITY: ....   **STATE:** ....

WENT WITH: **INITIAL IMPRESSION:**

....

WEATHER: **LENGTH OF STAY:**

....

EXPERIENCES/ OBSERVATIONS

FAVORITE MOMENT: ....

....

WILDLIFE SCENERY OBSERVED

....

....

....

PARK RATING 0/10

(1) (2) (3) (4) (5) (6) (7) (8) (9) (10)

WILL I VISIT AGAIN?   ◯ **YES**   ◯ **NO**

HIKING TRAIL: ....

LOCATION: ....

DATE: .... **DISTANCE:** ....

COMPANIONS: ....

WEATHER:

TRAIL DIFFICULTY:

TEMPERATURE: ....

① ② ③ ④ ⑤

THOUGHTS ABOUT THIS HIKE

....

....

....

....

....

....

....

OVERALL RATING

☆ ☆ ☆ ☆ ☆

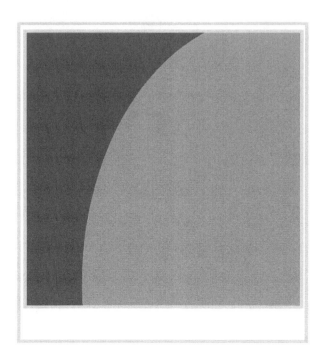

NOTES-MEMORIES-PHOTOS

....

....

....

....

....

....

....

....

....

....

SOUVENIRS TICKET STUBS MAPS MORE PICS

PARK VISIT # ▢ DATE: ....

NATIONAL PARK: ....

CITY: .... **STATE:** ....

WENT WITH: **INITIAL IMPRESSION:**

....

WEATHER: **LENGTH OF STAY:**

....

EXPERIENCES/ OBSERVATIONS

FAVORITE MOMENT: ....

....

WILDLIFE SCENERY OBSERVED

....

....

....

PARK RATING 0/10

① ② ③ ④ ⑤ ⑥ ⑦ ⑧ ⑨ ⑩

WILL I VISIT AGAIN? ⬭ YES ⬭ NO

HIKING TRAIL: ....

LOCATION: ....

DATE: .... **DISTANCE:** ....

COMPANIONS: ....

WEATHER:

TRAIL DIFFICULTY:

TEMPERATURE: ....

① ② ③ ④ ⑤

THOUGHTS ABOUT THIS HIKE

....
....
....
....
....
....
....

OVERALL RATING

☆ ☆ ☆ ☆ ☆

NOTES-MEMORIES-PHOTOS

....

....

....

....

....

....

....

....

....

....

SOUVENIRS TICKET STUBS MAPS MORE PICS

PARK VISIT # ☐ DATE: ....

NATIONAL PARK: ....

CITY: .... **STATE:** ....

WENT WITH: **INITIAL IMPRESSION:**

....

WEATHER: **LENGTH OF STAY:**

....

EXPERIENCES/ OBSERVATIONS

FAVORITE MOMENT: ....

....

WILDLIFE SCENERY OBSERVED

....

....

....

PARK RATING 0/10

① ② ③ ④ ⑤ ⑥ ⑦ ⑧ ⑨ ⑩
1   2   3   4   5   6   7   8   9   10

WILL I VISIT AGAIN? ◯ YES ◯ NO

HIKING TRAIL: ....

LOCATION: ....

DATE: .... **DISTANCE:** ....

COMPANIONS: ....

WEATHER:

TRAIL DIFFICULTY:

☉☀ ☉☁ ☉🌧

TEMPERATURE: ....

① ② ③ ④ ⑤

THOUGHTS ABOUT THIS HIKE

....

....

....

....

....

....

....

OVERALL RATING

☆ ☆ ☆ ☆ ☆

NOTES-MEMORIES-PHOTOS

....

....

....

....

....

....

....

....

....

....

SOUVENIRS TICKET STUBS MAPS MORE PICS

PARK VISIT # ☐   DATE: ....

NATIONAL PARK: ....

CITY: ....   **STATE:** ....

WENT WITH: **INITIAL IMPRESSION:**

....

WEATHER: **LENGTH OF STAY:**

....

EXPERIENCES/ OBSERVATIONS

FAVORITE MOMENT: ....

....

WILDLIFE SCENERY OBSERVED

....

....

....

PARK RATING 0/10

(1) (2) (3) (4) (5) (6) (7) (8) (9) (10)

WILL I VISIT AGAIN?   ◯ YES   ◯ NO

HIKING TRAIL: ....

LOCATION: ....

DATE: ....   **DISTANCE:** ....

COMPANIONS: ....

WEATHER:

⬭☀ ⬭☁ ⬭🌧

TEMPERATURE: ....

TRAIL DIFFICULTY:

(1) (2) (3) (4) (5)

THOUGHTS ABOUT THIS HIKE

....

....

....

....

....

....

....

OVERALL RATING

☆ ☆ ☆ ☆ ☆

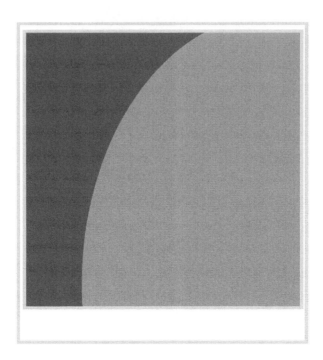

NOTES-MEMORIES-PHOTOS

....

....

....

....

....

....

....

....

....

....

SOUVENIRS TICKET STUBS MAPS MORE PICS

PARK VISIT # ⬭ DATE: ....

NATIONAL PARK: ....

CITY: .... **STATE:** ....

WENT WITH: **INITIAL IMPRESSION:**

....

WEATHER: **LENGTH OF STAY:**

....

EXPERIENCES/ OBSERVATIONS

FAVORITE MOMENT: ....

....

WILDLIFE SCENERY OBSERVED

....

....

....

PARK RATING 0/10

(1) (2) (3) (4) (5) (6) (7) (8) (9) (10)

WILL I VISIT AGAIN?   ⬭ YES   ⬭ NO

HIKING TRAIL: ....

LOCATION: ....

DATE: .... **DISTANCE:** ....

COMPANIONS: ....

WEATHER:

☀ ⛅ 🌧

TEMPERATURE: ....

TRAIL DIFFICULTY:

① ② ③ ④ ⑤

THOUGHTS ABOUT THIS HIKE

....

....

....

....

....

....

....

OVERALL RATING

☆ ☆ ☆ ☆ ☆

NOTES-MEMORIES-PHOTOS

....

....

....

....

....

....

....

....

....

....

SOUVENIRS TICKET STUBS MAPS MORE PICS

PARK VISIT # [   ]   DATE: ....

NATIONAL PARK: ....

CITY: ....   **STATE:** ....

WENT WITH: **INITIAL IMPRESSION:**

....

WEATHER: **LENGTH OF STAY:**

....

EXPERIENCES/ OBSERVATIONS

FAVORITE MOMENT: ....

....

WILDLIFE SCENERY OBSERVED

....

....

....

PARK RATING 0/10

(1) (2) (3) (4) (5) (6) (7) (8) (9) (10)

WILL I VISIT AGAIN?   ◯ YES   ◯ NO

HIKING TRAIL: ....

LOCATION: ....

DATE: .... **DISTANCE:** ....

COMPANIONS: ....

WEATHER: TRAIL DIFFICULTY:

○ ☀   ○ ☁   ○ 🌧

TEMPERATURE: ....   ① ② ③ ④ ⑤

THOUGHTS ABOUT THIS HIKE

....

....

....

....

....

....

....

OVERALL RATING

☆ ☆ ☆ ☆ ☆

NOTES-MEMORIES-PHOTOS

....

....

....

....

....

....

....

....

....

....

SOUVENIRS TICKET STUBS MAPS MORE PICS

PARK VISIT # ☐   DATE: ....

NATIONAL PARK: ....

CITY: ....   **STATE:** ....

WENT WITH: **INITIAL IMPRESSION:**

....

WEATHER: **LENGTH OF STAY:**

....

EXPERIENCES/ OBSERVATIONS

FAVORITE MOMENT: ....

....

WILDLIFE SCENERY OBSERVED

....

....

....

PARK RATING 0/10

① ② ③ ④ ⑤ ⑥ ⑦ ⑧ ⑨ ⑩

WILL I VISIT AGAIN?   ◯ YES   ◯ NO

HIKING TRAIL:
....

LOCATION:
....

DATE: ....   DISTANCE: ....

COMPANIONS:
....

WEATHER:

☁ ☀ ☁ ☁ ☁ 🌧

TRAIL DIFFICULTY:

TEMPERATURE: ....

(1) (2) (3) (4) (5)

THOUGHTS ABOUT THIS HIKE

....

....

....

....

....

....

....

OVERALL RATING
☆ ☆ ☆ ☆ ☆

NOTES-MEMORIES-PHOTOS

....

....

....

....

....

....

....

....

....

....

SOUVENIRS TICKET STUBS MAPS MORE PICS

PARK VISIT # [   ]   DATE: ....

NATIONAL PARK: ....

CITY: ....   **STATE:** ....

WENT WITH: **INITIAL IMPRESSION:**

....

WEATHER: **LENGTH OF STAY:**

....

EXPERIENCES/ OBSERVATIONS

FAVORITE MOMENT: ....

....

WILDLIFE SCENERY OBSERVED

....

....

....

PARK RATING 0/10

(1) (2) (3) (4) (5) (6) (7) (8) (9) (10)

WILL I VISIT AGAIN?   ◯ YES   ◯ NO

HIKING TRAIL: ....

LOCATION: ....

DATE: .... **DISTANCE:** ....

COMPANIONS: ....

WEATHER:

○ ☀ ○ ☁ ○ 🌧

TEMPERATURE: ....

TRAIL DIFFICULTY:

(1) (2) (3) (4) (5)

THOUGHTS ABOUT THIS HIKE

....

....

....

....

....

....

....

OVERALL RATING

☆ ☆ ☆ ☆ ☆

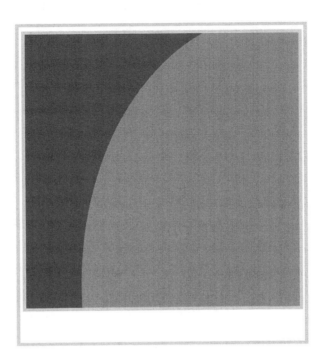

NOTES-MEMORIES-PHOTOS

....

....

....

....

....

....

....

....

....

....

SOUVENIRS TICKET STUBS MAPS MORE PICS

PARK VISIT # ☐ DATE: ....

NATIONAL PARK: ....

CITY: .... **STATE:** ....

WENT WITH:

....

WEATHER:

....

INITIAL IMPRESSION:

....

LENGTH OF STAY:

....

EXPERIENCES/ OBSERVATIONS

FAVORITE MOMENT: ....

....

WILDLIFE SCENERY OBSERVED

....

....

....

PARK RATING 0/10

(1) (2) (3) (4) (5) (6) (7) (8) (9) (10)

WILL I VISIT AGAIN? ◯ YES ◯ NO

HIKING TRAIL: ....

LOCATION: ....

DATE: ....   **DISTANCE:** ....

COMPANIONS: ....

WEATHER:

⬭☀ ⬭☁ ⬭🌧

TRAIL DIFFICULTY:

TEMPERATURE: ....   ① ② ③ ④ ⑤

THOUGHTS ABOUT THIS HIKE

....

....

....

....

....

....

....

OVERALL RATING

☆☆☆☆☆

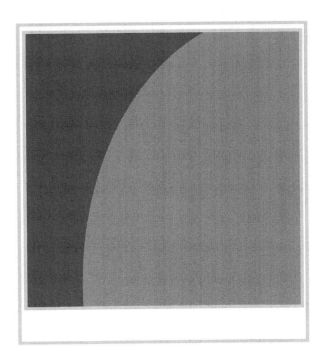

NOTES-MEMORIES-PHOTOS

....

....

....

....

....

....

....

....

....

....

SOUVENIRS TICKET STUBS MAPS MORE PICS

PARK VISIT # [   ]   DATE: ....

NATIONAL PARK: ....

CITY: ....   **STATE:** ....

WENT WITH: **INITIAL IMPRESSION:**

....

WEATHER: **LENGTH OF STAY:**

....

EXPERIENCES/ OBSERVATIONS

FAVORITE MOMENT: ....

....

WILDLIFE SCENERY OBSERVED

....

....

....

PARK RATING 0/10

(1) (2) (3) (4) (5) (6) (7) (8) (9) (10)

WILL I VISIT AGAIN?   ◯ YES   ◯ NO

HIKING TRAIL: ....

LOCATION: ....

DATE: ....   **DISTANCE:** ....

COMPANIONS: ....

WEATHER:

TRAIL DIFFICULTY:

TEMPERATURE: ....   ① ② ③ ④ ⑤

THOUGHTS ABOUT THIS HIKE

....

....

....

....

....

....

....

OVERALL RATING

☆ ☆ ☆ ☆ ☆

NOTES-MEMORIES-PHOTOS

....

....

....

....

....

....

....

....

....

....

SOUVENIRS TICKET STUBS MAPS MORE PICS

PARK VISIT # ⬚   DATE: ....

NATIONAL PARK: ....

CITY: ....   **STATE:** ....

WENT WITH: **INITIAL IMPRESSION:**

....

WEATHER: **LENGTH OF STAY:**

....

EXPERIENCES/ OBSERVATIONS

FAVORITE MOMENT: ....

....

WILDLIFE SCENERY OBSERVED

....

....

....

PARK RATING 0/10

(1) (2) (3) (4) (5) (6) (7) (8) (9) (10)

WILL I VISIT AGAIN?   ◯ YES   ◯ NO

HIKING TRAIL: ....

LOCATION: ....

DATE: .... **DISTANCE:** ....

COMPANIONS: ....

WEATHER:

☀ ○ ☁ ○ 🌧

TEMPERATURE: ....

TRAIL DIFFICULTY:

1 2 3 4 5

THOUGHTS ABOUT THIS HIKE

....

....

....

....

....

....

....

OVERALL RATING

☆ ☆ ☆ ☆ ☆

NOTES-MEMORIES-PHOTOS

....

....

....

....

....

....

....

....

....

....

SOUVENIRS TICKET STUBS MAPS MORE PICS

PARK VISIT # ☐   DATE: ....

NATIONAL PARK: ....

CITY: ....   **STATE:** ....

WENT WITH: **INITIAL IMPRESSION:**

....

WEATHER: **LENGTH OF STAY:**

....

EXPERIENCES/ OBSERVATIONS

FAVORITE MOMENT: ....

....

WILDLIFE SCENERY OBSERVED

....

....

....

PARK RATING 0/10

(1) (2) (3) (4) (5) (6) (7) (8) (9) (10)

WILL I VISIT AGAIN?   ◯ YES   ◯ NO

HIKING TRAIL: ....

LOCATION: ....

DATE: .... **DISTANCE:** ....

COMPANIONS: ....

WEATHER:

TRAIL DIFFICULTY:

TEMPERATURE: ....

$\textcircled{1}$ $\textcircled{2}$ $\textcircled{3}$ $\textcircled{4}$ $\textcircled{5}$

THOUGHTS ABOUT THIS HIKE

....

....

....

....

....

....

....

OVERALL RATING

☆ ☆ ☆ ☆ ☆

NOTES-MEMORIES-PHOTOS

....

....

....

....

....

....

....

....

....

....

SOUVENIRS TICKET STUBS MAPS MORE PICS

PARK VISIT # [ ]   DATE: ....

NATIONAL PARK: ....

CITY: ....   **STATE:** ....

WENT WITH: **INITIAL IMPRESSION:**

....

WEATHER: **LENGTH OF STAY:**

....

EXPERIENCES/ OBSERVATIONS

FAVORITE MOMENT: ....

....

WILDLIFE SCENERY OBSERVED

....

....

....

PARK RATING 0/10

(1) (2) (3) (4) (5) (6) (7) (8) (9) (10)

WILL I VISIT AGAIN?   ◯ YES   ◯ NO

HIKING TRAIL: ....

LOCATION: ....

DATE: ....   **DISTANCE:** ....

COMPANIONS: ....

WEATHER:

TRAIL DIFFICULTY:

TEMPERATURE: ....   (1) (2) (3) (4) (5)

THOUGHTS ABOUT THIS HIKE

....

....

....

....

....

....

....

OVERALL RATING

☆ ☆ ☆ ☆ ☆

NOTES-MEMORIES-PHOTOS

....

....

....

....

....

....

....

....

....

....

SOUVENIRS TICKET STUBS MAPS MORE PICS

PARK VISIT # ⬚ **DATE:** ....

NATIONAL PARK: ....

CITY: .... **STATE:** ....

WENT WITH: **INITIAL IMPRESSION:**

....

WEATHER: **LENGTH OF STAY:**

....

EXPERIENCES/ OBSERVATIONS

FAVORITE MOMENT: ....

....

WILDLIFE SCENERY OBSERVED

....

....

....

PARK RATING 0/10

(1) (2) (3) (4) (5) (6) (7) (8) (9) (10)

WILL I VISIT AGAIN?   ◯ **YES**   ◯ **NO**

HIKING TRAIL: ....

LOCATION: ....

DATE: ....   **DISTANCE:** ....

COMPANIONS: ....

WEATHER: **TRAIL DIFFICULTY:**

TEMPERATURE: ....   ① ② ③ ④ ⑤

THOUGHTS ABOUT THIS HIKE

....

....

....

....

....

....

....

OVERALL RATING

☆ ☆ ☆ ☆ ☆

NOTES-MEMORIES-PHOTOS

....

....

....

....

....

....

....

....

....

....

SOUVENIRS TICKET STUBS MAPS MORE PICS

PARK VISIT # [ ] DATE: ....

NATIONAL PARK: ....

CITY: .... **STATE:** ....

WENT WITH: **INITIAL IMPRESSION:**

....

WEATHER: **LENGTH OF STAY:**

....

EXPERIENCES/ OBSERVATIONS

FAVORITE MOMENT: ....

....

WILDLIFE SCENERY OBSERVED

....

....

....

PARK RATING 0/10

(1) (2) (3) (4) (5) (6) (7) (8) (9) (10)

WILL I VISIT AGAIN?   ◯ YES   ◯ NO

HIKING TRAIL: ....

LOCATION: ....

DATE: .... **DISTANCE:** ....

COMPANIONS: ....

WEATHER:

☁ ☀   ☁ ☁   ☁ 🌧

TRAIL DIFFICULTY:

(1) (2) (3) (4) (5)

TEMPERATURE: ....

THOUGHTS ABOUT THIS HIKE

....

....

....

....

....

....

....

OVERALL RATING

☆ ☆ ☆ ☆ ☆

NOTES-MEMORIES-PHOTOS

....

....

....

....

....

....

....

....

....

....

SOUVENIRS TICKET STUBS MAPS MORE PICS

PARK VISIT # ☐ DATE: ....

NATIONAL PARK: ....

CITY: .... **STATE:** ....

WENT WITH: **INITIAL IMPRESSION:**

....

WEATHER: **LENGTH OF STAY:**

....

EXPERIENCES/ OBSERVATIONS

FAVORITE MOMENT: ....

....

WILDLIFE SCENERY OBSERVED

....

....

....

PARK RATING 0/10

(1) (2) (3) (4) (5) (6) (7) (8) (9) (10)

WILL I VISIT AGAIN?   ◯ YES   ◯ NO

HIKING TRAIL: ....

LOCATION: ....

DATE: .... DISTANCE: ....

COMPANIONS: ....

WEATHER:

TRAIL DIFFICULTY:

◯ ☀ ◯ ☁ ◯ 🌧

TEMPERATURE: ....

1 2 3 4 5

THOUGHTS ABOUT THIS HIKE

....

....

....

....

....

....

....

OVERALL RATING

☆ ☆ ☆ ☆ ☆

NOTES-MEMORIES-PHOTOS

....

....

....

....

....

....

....

....

....

....

SOUVENIRS TICKET STUBS MAPS MORE PICS

PARK VISIT # ☐   DATE: ....

NATIONAL PARK: ....

CITY: ....   **STATE:** ....

WENT WITH: **INITIAL IMPRESSION:**

....

WEATHER: **LENGTH OF STAY:**

....

EXPERIENCES/ OBSERVATIONS

FAVORITE MOMENT: ....

....

WILDLIFE SCENERY OBSERVED

....

....

....

PARK RATING 0/10

(1) (2) (3) (4) (5) (6) (7) (8) (9) (10)

WILL I VISIT AGAIN?   ⬯ YES   ⬯ NO

HIKING TRAIL: ....

LOCATION: ....

DATE: ....   **DISTANCE:** ....

COMPANIONS: ....

WEATHER:

TEMPERATURE: ....

TRAIL DIFFICULTY:

(1) (2) (3) (4) (5)

THOUGHTS ABOUT THIS HIKE

....

....

....

....

....

....

....

OVERALL RATING

☆ ☆ ☆ ☆ ☆

NOTES-MEMORIES-PHOTOS

....

....

....

....

....

....

....

....

....

....

SOUVENIRS TICKET STUBS MAPS MORE PICS

PARK VISIT # ☐   DATE: ....

NATIONAL PARK: ....

CITY: ....   **STATE:** ....

WENT WITH: **INITIAL IMPRESSION:**

....

WEATHER: **LENGTH OF STAY:**

....

EXPERIENCES/ OBSERVATIONS

FAVORITE MOMENT: ....

....

WILDLIFE SCENERY OBSERVED

....

....

....

PARK RATING 0/10

① ② ③ ④ ⑤ ⑥ ⑦ ⑧ ⑨ ⑩

WILL I VISIT AGAIN?   ◯ YES   ◯ NO

HIKING TRAIL: ....

LOCATION: ....

DATE: ....   **DISTANCE:** ....

COMPANIONS: ....

WEATHER:

TEMPERATURE: ....

TRAIL DIFFICULTY:

1 2 3 4 5

THOUGHTS ABOUT THIS HIKE

....

....

....

....

....

....

....

OVERALL RATING

☆ ☆ ☆ ☆ ☆

NOTES-MEMORIES-PHOTOS

....

....

....

....

....

....

....

....

....

....

SOUVENIRS TICKET STUBS MAPS MORE PICS

PARK VISIT # ⬚ DATE: ....

NATIONAL PARK: ....

CITY: .... **STATE:** ....

WENT WITH: **INITIAL IMPRESSION:**

....

WEATHER: **LENGTH OF STAY:**

....

EXPERIENCES/ OBSERVATIONS

FAVORITE MOMENT: ....

....

WILDLIFE SCENERY OBSERVED

....

....

....

PARK RATING 0/10

(1) (2) (3) (4) (5) (6) (7) (8) (9) (10)

WILL I VISIT AGAIN? ◯ YES ◯ NO

HIKING TRAIL: ....

LOCATION: ....

DATE: .... **DISTANCE:** ....

COMPANIONS: ....

WEATHER:

TRAIL DIFFICULTY:

TEMPERATURE: ....

① ② ③ ④ ⑤

THOUGHTS ABOUT THIS HIKE

....

....

....

....

....

....

....

OVERALL RATING

☆ ☆ ☆ ☆ ☆

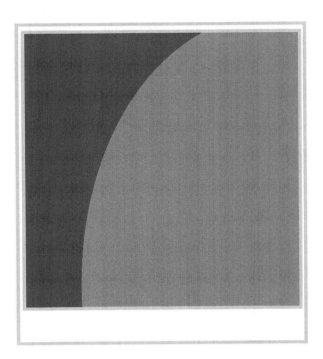

NOTES-MEMORIES-PHOTOS

....

....

....

....

....

....

....

....

....

....

SOUVENIRS TICKET STUBS MAPS MORE PICS

Made in the USA
Monee, IL
13 November 2020